ThiNkiNg Hats

Book 1

Anna Forsyth

Curriculum Concepts

comprehensive coverage

Thinking Hats

ISBN 9781906125561

Ordering Code – UK0150

Curriculum Concepts UK

The Old School

Upper High Street

Bedlinog

Mid-Glamorgan CF46 6SA

Email: orders@curriculumconcepts.co.uk

www.curriculumconcepts.co.uk

Contents

Introduction

Why Thinking Hats?

Have you ever heard the phrase, "Put your thinking caps on."? We often use it when faced with a situation that requires focused thinking. Whether it is a complex problem or a simple decision, there are many occasions when purposeful thinking is required. In an age of easy access to new information and technology, it is important to teach students not what to think, but *how* to think. In his book *Six Thinking Hats*, Edward De Bono* has created a six-hat system that trains students to focus their thinking for specific purposes, and to think in new ways, such as weighing up positive and negative outcomes and looking at the bigger picture. Each hat is a different colour, and represents a different way of thinking. This book is a collection of lessons that you can use in your classroom using the thinking hats concept. At the back of this book you will find a reference chart that explains the hats in more detail.

* De Bono, E. *Six Thinking Hats.*

Boston, Mass., U.S.A. Little, Brown and Company, (1st Back Pay paperback edition, rev. and updated.) 1999.

How to Use This Book

This book is divided into curriculum areas; Art, Music, PHSE and Citizenship, Physical Education, Geography, History, English, Design and Technology, Mathematics and Science. For most curriculum areas there are two easy-to-use lesson plans at two levels of difficulty – Year 1 and Year 2. Some lesson plans have more than one related curriculum area.

The lessons are suggestions only, and can be adapted to meet the needs of your students.

At the back of the book are templates (pages 43-49) that are required for the lessons;

- The Colour Wheel
  - cards with a picture of a hat with the colour and a graphic to assist with recognition,
  - cards for each hat with key questions to ask (to be photocopied onto the back of the hats)
- A Thinking Hats Reference Chart which summarises what each hat represents.
- A Hat template.
- Thinking Hats key words on cards to be photocopied.

As you become more confident with using the 'Thinking Hats' concept all these templates can be incorporated into everyday activities. The more your students use the Thinking Hats concept the better their thinking skills will become.

When introducing the hats, it is best to teach them as a separate unit before incorporating them in to other areas. For younger children, consider introducing each hat separately so they understand what each hat means/represents and what they have to think about. Before you begin, take the time to read the Thinking Hats Reference Chart at the back of this book and familiarise yourself with the six hats.

Teachers will need to give some forethought into the amount of supervision, guidance and teacher participation given to help students work through the activities in the series. Students' ages and abilities will play a factor in these and the degree to which students are to work independently. Happy thinking!

My Favourite

Subject: PHSE: Music Dance

Teacher's Notes

Year: 1

Group/Class Size: Any
Duration: 15-20 minutes

Lesson Objective(s):

* Students will explore through movement the dance elements of body awareness, space, time, energy, and relationships.

Learning Outcomes:

* Students will explore body awareness through music by using thinking hats to explore the ways they move to different types of music.

Write your own learning outcome(s) here:

Point(s) to Ponder:

* The white hat may not suit this activity.
* The time frame for this lesson is a suggestion only.

You will need:

* Colour wheel or thinking hats cards
* Recordings of contrasting music eg. classical/jazz/hip hop/rock
* Whiteboard and markers or large sheet of paper

Activity

★ Play three different types of music. Explore different ways of moving to each style, such as fast and jumpy, or slow and fluid. Students experiment to see what movement fits the music best.

★ As a class, pull out a thinking hat card or spin the thinking hat wheel.

★ Use the thinking hat to talk about how different music makes you move. For example:

Black hat: The song was too jumpy, and it was too hard to dance to.

Red hat: The first song made me feel sad, so I moved slowly.

★ If time permits, repeat with three more contrasting pieces of music or carry on more discussion with different thinking hats.

Follow the Leader

Teacher's Notes

Group/Class Size: 4 groups
Duration: 15-20 minutes

Lesson Objective(s):
* Students will share movement through informal presentation and respond personally to their own and others' dance.

Learning Outcomes:
* Students will share movements with each other and respond by adding to the movement that has been given.
* Students will use thinking hats to critique their own and others' dancing.

Write your own learning outcome(s) here:

Point(s) to Ponder:
* Group size may vary depending on the class size, the age of the students and their ability to work in a group setting.

You will need:
* Thinking hats cards or wheel
* Comfortable dancing shoes
* Some older children to lead the groups (Maybe a buddy class?)
* Music to move to

Activity

★ Split the class into groups of 4 or more.

★ Play the music. Students make up a short movement each.

★ They teach their movement to the rest of the group one by one.

★ Each group will have a dance made up of each student's movement. They practise the dance as a group.

★ Groups take turns to show their dance to the class.

★ Pick a thinking hat card or spin the wheel.

★ Discuss each dance using the thinking hats after each performance.

   White hat: What moves did they do?

   Yellow hat: What did they do well?

   Green hat: How could they make it different?

★ Repeat activity again if time allows.

Slice of Life

Subject: PHSE: Music Dance

Year: 2

Teacher's Notes

Group/Class Size: In Groups
Duration: 15-20 minutes

Lesson Objective(s):
* Students will initiate and express dance ideas based on a variety of stimuli.

Learning Outcome(s):
* Students will use thinking hats to express dance ideas based on viewing a short dance sequence.

Write your own learning outcome(s) here:

Point(s) to Ponder:
* With this activity, questions for each hat need to be prepared beforehand.

You will need:
* Thinking hats cards or wheel
* A brief video clip or live performance of a dance sequence
* Music of your choice
* Large sheet of paper or whiteboard and pens
* Question preprepared

Activity

★ Play a short dance sequence to the class (this could be video or live performance).

★ Pick a thinking hat card or spin the wheel.

★ Discuss the dance using the thinking hats:

Green hat: How could we change this dance?
What could they do next?

Red hat: How did you feel about that dance?

Repeat with a different dance if you have time.

Dance Around the World

Teacher's notes

Subject: PHSE: Dance and Music
Geography   **Year:** 2

Group/Class Size: Any
Duration: 20-30 minutes

Lesson Objective(s):

* Students will demonstrate an awareness of dance as part of community life.

Learning Outcomes:

* Students will use thinking hats to discuss what they know about dance in different cultural communities from around the world using videos and photos.

Write your own learning outcome(s) here:

Point(s) to Ponder:

* This would be a great opportunity for students to show examples of dance from their own cultures to their class.

You will need:

* Thinking hats cards or wheel
* Videos, pictures or example of dance from a variety of cultures

Activity

★ Watch videos or look at pictures of dance from different cultures.

★ Pick thinking hats cards or spin the wheel.

★ Use the hats to discuss dance in different cultures:

Red hat: How do you think this person feels about dance?

Yellow hat: What are the positive things about dance in this community? What do you like about dance in this culture?

Green hat: What is unusual or creative or different about this dance?

★ Repeat with different thinking hats/different cultures.

Take Two

Subject: English: Drama

Teacher's Notes

Year: 1

Group/Class Size: Whole class, then in groups
Duration: 15-20 minutes

Lesson Objective(s):
• Students will contribute ideas and participate in drama, using personal experiences and imagination.

Learning Outcomes:
• Students will participate in drama, using imagination and thinking hats to re-create a scene.

Write your own learning outcome(s) here:

Point(s) to Ponder:
• This is a theatre-sports activity which is best done as a whole class, then in groups, so that students can see the game in action.

You will need:
• Thinking hats cards with the white hat card removed
• Props or costumes if desired

Activity

★ Do this game as a whole class first, then in groups.

★ Choose three people to act out a scene.

★ Ask the audience to give the following:

a place or location, a problem or situation, a character or job.

★ Actors: create a short scene using the given scenario.

★ Get one audience member to pick a thinking hats card or spin the wheel.

★ Actors: re-create the scene using the thinking hats:

Blue hat: Bigger picture. Create a new location or problem entirely.

Red hat: Emotion. A different feeling or emotion.

Green hat: Create a different twist or ending.

White hat: Do not use this hat for this activity.

Yellow hat: Look at the positive. Create a happy ending, or a positive outcome.

Black hat: Look at the negative. Create a sad or negative ending or outcome to the problem.

★ Take turns at acting or being in the audience.

You Be the Judge

Teacher's Notes

Group/Class Size: Whole class or in groups
Duration: 20-30 minutes

Lesson Objective(s):

* Students will share drama through informal presentation and respond to ways in which drama tells stories and conveys ideas.

Learning Outcomes:

* Students will act out a short scene from a chosen fairy tale (from a book), such as *The Three Little Pigs* or a story of choice.
* Students will respond to the ideas in the drama using thinking hats.

Write your own learning outcome(s) here:

Point(s) to Ponder:

* This activity could be introduced as a whole class first, then in groups, depending on the age and ability of the students.

You will need:

* Thinking hats cards or wheel
* A short scene from a well-known story, fairy tale or nursery rhyme
* Props and costumes if desired.

Activity

* ★ Choose a scene from a well-known story, fairy tale or nursery rhyme.
* ★ For this activity you will need 3 actors, 3 judges and an audience.
* ★ Actors: Go and practise the scene.
* ★ Pick a thinking hat card or spin the wheel to pick a hat. Judges: take turns being the audience if working in groups.
* ★ Judge using each hat as follows:

  White hat: What did they do with their bodies/faces/placement/movements?

  Red hat: What emotions did they show?

  Yellow hat: What did they do well?

  Black hat: What was one movement/part that they had problems with?

  Green hat: What could they do next time to make it better or more interesting?

  Blue hat: How was their drama overall? What was your impression of their drama generally?

* ★ Switch roles and repeat.

Dear Diary . . .

Subject: English: Drama

Year: 2

Teacher's Notes

Group/Class Size: Whole class, then in groups
Duration: 20-30 minutes

Lesson Objective(s):
* Students will contribute and develop ideas in drama based on personal experience, imagination and other stimuli.

Learning Outcomes:
* Students will create a short drama based on their personal experiences, using the thinking hats as a starting point.

Write your own learning outcome(s) here:

Point(s) to Ponder:
* It is best to choose three confident students to demostrate in front of the whole class first, then repeat the activity in groups.

You will need:
* Thinking hats cards with blue and white hats removed
* Props or costumes if desired

Activity

★ Pick three people to act out a short scene.

★ Each actor: pick a thinking hat card or spin the wheel. The white hat and the blue hat are not needed for this activity.

★ Using the thinking hats, think of an experience:

> **Red hat:** A time when they felt sad/happy/scared/bored/a really strong emotion.
>
> **Black hat:** When something awful happened.
>
> **Yellow hat:** When something positive happened.
>
> **Green hat:** Make up an experience from your imagination.

★ Actors: create a scene using the three experiences put together.

★ Discuss the activity and have students repeat the activity in small groups.

★ Take turns at acting and sharing your scenes in front of the class.

Back To the Future

Subject: English: Drama

Year: 2

Teacher's Notes

Group/Class Size: Whole class, then groups
Duration: 20-30 minutes

Lesson Objective(s):
- Students will contribute and develop ideas in drama based on personal experience, imagination and other stimuli.
- Students will share drama through informal presentation and respond to elements of drama.

Learning Outcomes:
- Students will contribute and develop ideas of alternative endings to a story or drama using yellow, black, green and red thinking hats.
- Students will share dramas with their class in an informal setting.

Write your own learning outcome(s) here:

You will need:
- Thinking hats cards: green, yellow, black and red
- Props or costumes if desired.
- A list of topics, such as the zoo, fitness or the supermarket.

Activity

- ★ List some topics on the board.
- ★ Create a short dramatic scene on a topic of choice. (This is better in small groups, but could be done as a class first.)
- ★ In your group, pick one of the topics. Talk and walk it through.
- ★ Act out the scene.
- ★ Pick a thinking hat card or spin the thinking hat wheel.
- ★ Using the thinking hats, create a scene that would continue on from where you left off like so:

  Red hat: How would the person feel or react to what just happened? How would they react next?

  Green hat: What could happen that might be unexpected?

  Yellow hat: What positive thing might happen next?

  Black hat: What could go wrong?

- ★ Try picking different thinking hats and coming up with lots of new endings or extra scenes.

Music Mania

Subject: Music

Year: 1

Teacher's Notes

Group/Class Size: Any size
Duration: 15-20 minutes

Lesson Objective(s):
* Students will identify music as part of everyday life and recognise that it serves a variety of purposes.

Learning Outcomes:
* Students will identify aspects of music in their own lives and discuss using the thinking hats.

Write your own learning outcome(s) here:

Point(s) to Ponder:
* You may wish to leave the blue hat out of this activity at this level.

You will need:
* Thinking hats cards or wheel
* Large sheets of coloured paper for class chart

Activity

★ Draw up a class chart with a section for each coloured hat.

★ Write a word or phrase under each coloured hat section, to indicate to students what is required for each, such as;

Yellow hat: Positive or things I like/favourite music.

White hat: What I know about music.

Red hat: Feelings/Moods.

Black hat: Music I don't like/ things about music that are negative.

Blue hat: What is music? Different types of music.

★ Take turns at picking a card or spinning the wheel.

★ Give one point from each chosen hat and write it on the shared chart.

★ Fill it in as a class.

★ Decorate and display the class music chart with music pictures and musical notes.

★ Discuss what you have learned about music.

Music Idol

Teacher's Notes

Group/Class Size: Any
Duration: 15-20 minutes

Lesson Objective(s):

- Students will share music making with others through informal presentation and respond to live or recorded music.

Learning Outcomes:

- Students will watch videos of singers or musicians or hear them live and respond using the thinking hats.

Write your own learning outcome(s) here:

You will need:

- Thinking hats cards or wheel
- Videos of musical auditions or performances if available or students from the class willing to show their performance for the class.

Activity

★ Watch short musical performances.

★ Choose a thinking hat card or spin the wheel.

★ Use the thinking hats to discuss the performances:

Yellow Hat: What did they do well?

White Hat: Information or facts about the performance. What did they do?

Green Hat: What could they do differently next time?

Black Hat: What did they do wrong? (Your turn to be the judge!)

Blue Hat: How would you rate their performance overall? Did you like it as a whole?

★ Repeat with a different performance.

Chance Music

Subject: Music

Teacher's Notes

Year: 2

Group/Class Size: Groups of 4 or 5
Duration: 15-20 minutes

Lesson Objective(s):
- Students will invent and represent musical ideas, drawing on imagination and responding to sources of motivation.

Learning Outcomes:
- Students will invent a musical idea using an assortment of simple percussion instruments, using their imagination and the thinking hats.

Write your own learning outcome(s) here:

Point(s) to Ponder:
- If you don't have a variety of instruments on hand, you could make your own or use body percussion.
- This activity can be very noisy. You have been warned! Students may need a rule of taking turns to show their sounds to the group. No playing all at once!

You will need:
- Thinking hats cards or wheel
- An assortment of percussion instruments such as: a triangle, maracas, castanets, small drums, tambourines or any other instruments of choice
- A big dose of imagination and a desire to have fun!

Activity

- ★ Split into groups of 4 or 5.
- ★ Each group: Take a thinking hats wheel or a set of thinking hats cards and a box of instruments.
- ★ Use the hats as follows:

    Yellow hat: Make a sound that you like or a nice sound.

    Black hat: Make a sound that you hate or a terrible/horrible/ugly sound.

    Red hat: Think of a sound that makes you feel happy, sad, angry or another emotion.

    Green hat: Make the craziest, most creative/weirdest sound you can make.

    White hat: Tell the class what you did to make your song.

    Blue hat: Give your sound or song a name. Think about what the song is about/the feeling you get from it.

- ★ Put the sounds together to make a small piece of music.
- ★ Keep picking cards until the teacher tells you to stop.
- ★ Perform your piece to the class.
- ★ Remember – be creative!

Soundtrax

Subject: Music
Year: 2

Teacher's Notes

Group/Class Size: Whole class
Duration: 30-40 Minutes

Lesson Objective(s):

• Students will identify music as part of everyday life and recognise that it serves a variety of purposes.

Learning Outcomes:

• Students will investigate music as a soundtrack to a cartoon and recognise its purpose of enhancing the visual and creating an atmosphere, using thinking hats to stimulate discussion.

Write your own learning outcome(s) here:

Point(s) to Ponder:

• You may like to use the hats for discussion at different stages, such as when the music has been played with the clip.

You will need:

• Thinking hats cards or wheel
• A short scene from a cartoon or movie
• Several contrasting pieces of music

Activity

★ Watch the clip without any sound.

★ Think about what happens and use the hats to discuss as follows:

Red hat: What emotions can you see? How do you think the characters feel?

Blue hat: What is it all about? What is the main thing that happens?

White hat: What are the facts? What can you see? What happens/to who/where are they/what are they doing?

Yellow hat: What happens that is happy or positive?

Black hat: Did anything negative happen?

Green hat: Can you think of any music already that might suit the clip?

★ What instruments or noises do you think you could use for the soundtrack?

★ Watch the clip again a couple of times.

★ Play each piece of music and discuss which one would suit the clip and why, using the thinking hats.

★ Choose the best piece of music and play it along with the clip.

★ Discuss: Did it work? Why or why not?

★ If you have time, you could make up your own music.

The Birthday Party

Teacher's Notes

Group/Class Size: Any size
Duration: 15-20 minutes

Lesson Objective(s):

* Students will express ideas about their own work and respond to objects and images made by others.

Learning Outcomes:

* Students will create art works using a variety of different media to express ideas about a birthday party using thinking hats as motivation.

Write your own learning outcome(s) here:

Point(s) to Ponder:

* You may wish to put up a display or chart of what different hats mean during the activity for easy reference.
* You may wish to look at stories, pictures or clips of different birthday parties for inspiration.
* Choose different types of art such as collage, line drawings or painting.

You will need:

* Thinking hats cards or wheel
* Art paper
* Photos, pictures or stories about birthday parties
* Crayons, chalk or coloured pencils
* Magazines, coloured card, glitter etc.

* ★ Discuss birthday parties you have been to and what happened.
* ★ Using the thinking hats, come up with some ideas for art work and do one as a class.
* ★ Use the hats as follows:

  Red hat: How did different people at the party feel? How can we show that in our picture?

  Yellow hat: What is something really positive or fun about birthday parties? Let's put that in our picture.

  Black hat: What is something negative that might happen at a birthday party? Has anything you didn't like ever happened at a party that you have been to?

  White hat: Get the facts. What things do we normally see at a party? Balloons or presents? Pin the tail on the donkey?

  Green hat: Get creative. What is something weird or strange that could happen at a birthday party? Maybe a spaceship lands in the back yard?

  Blue hat: Let's look at the whole picture and how it all goes together.

* ★ Allocate different hats to different groups, or get students to use as many hats as they can to help them draw their picture.
* ★ Use whatever medium you choose to create pictures on the theme of birthday parties. These make a great classroom display.

Art Detective

Teacher's Notes

Group/Class Size: Any
Duration: 15-20 minutes

Lesson Objective(s):
* Students will identify objects and images in everyday life and recognise that they serve a variety of purposes.

Learning Outcomes:
* Students will identify images and objects of art in the classroom and discuss using thinking hats.

Write your own learning outcome(s) here:

Point(s) to Ponder:
* How about a prize for the most interesting object or image?
* Objects or images could include cartoons, designs, photographs or patterns. Give students some examples to get them started.

You will need:
* Thinking hats cards or wheel
* Art images or objects planted around the classroom

Activity

* ★ Put the stopwatch on. You have 2–3 minutes to find one art object or image from around the classroom. Keep it a secret!

* ★ Freeze or sit down when the timer stops.

* ★ What did you find? Point out findings to the class.

* ★ A walk around the class might be fun, pointing out what each person found along the way.

Use the thinking hats to discuss the most interesting objects or images as follows:

Yellow hat: What do you like about this object/image?

Black hat: What don't you like about this object/image?

Blue hat: Where does this image or object come from originally? What is the context?

White hat: What is it? Is it a painting? What does it mean? What can you see?

Green hat: What else could you use it for? How could you make it different?

* ★ Hand out prizes or try to be an art detective in another classroom or outside.

Walk of Art

Subject: Art

Year: 2

Teacher's Notes

Group/Class Size: Any
Duration: 15-20 minutes

Lesson Objective(s):
* Students will describe ways in which objects and images can communicate stories and ideas.

Learning Outcomes:
* Students will use thinking hats to describe the ideas or stories in a variety of art images.

Write your own learning outcome(s) here:

Point(s) to Ponder:
* Reading abilities within the class may differ, so it would be helpful to walk the trail with the students first and read each question out loud together.
* Keep an eye out for students who may struggle with reading and keep it simple.
* This activity could be great on a trip to the art gallery.
* Mix up the general mediums and eras of the art works where possible.

You will need:
* Thinking hats questions, cards or wheel
* A variety of contrasting art works
* An art trail (Be creative.)

Activity

★ Set up a walk of art in your classroom, by sticking contrasting pieces of art up in different locations.

★ Stick a simple thinking hat question under each one (or key word).
Here are some examples:

Red hat: How does it make you feel? What emotions can you see?

White hat: What shapes/objects/images can you see in this picture?

Green hat: What would you change about this picture? If you could do another artwork to follow on from this one, what would you do? What do you think might happen next?

Yellow hat: What do you like about this piece?

Black hat: What do you dislike about this piece?

Blue hat: What is the main point of this artwork?

★ Once everyone has done the art walk at their own pace, come together as a class or re-walk the track and discuss.

Thinking Hat Display

Subject: Art

Year: 2

Teacher's Notes

Group/Class Size: Whole class then 6 groups
Duration: 15-20 minutes

Lesson Objective(s):
• Students will develop visual ideas in response to a variety of motivations, using imagination, observation, and invention with materials.

Learning Outcomes:
• Students will develop visual ideas in a class display in response to thinking hats, using their imagination.

Write your own learning outcome(s) here:

Point(s) to Ponder:
• This is a great way of incorporating the thinking hats system into your classroom environment.

You will need:
• Thinking hats chart for reference
• Coloured paper or magazines
• Glue
• Coloured pencils, crayons or paint
• Hat template (see the back of this book)
• Large sheets of paper

Activity

★ Stick a large sheet of paper on one wall of your classroom with the title "Thinking Hats".

★ Divide the paper into six sections, one for each hat.

★ Draw or stick up ideas for each hat and discuss what each hat means. For example, you could put a sun for the yellow hat or a smiley face or maybe a present because it makes you happy.

★ Split into six groups with one thinking hat each.

★ Cut out pictures or draw images that match the colour of the hat you have been given.

★ Stick the images into each section of the class display. Ask students to tell the class about them and why you chose them.

★ Decorate and display in your classroom.

New Kid On the Block

Teacher's Notes

Group/Class Size: Whole class or in groups
Duration: 30-40 minutes. May need more than 1 lesson

Lesson Objective(s):
• Students will explore and share ideas about relationships with other people.

Learning Outcomes:
• Students will use digital media and thinking hats to explore and share ideas about building relationships in a new place.

Write your own learning outcome(s) here:

Point(s) to Ponder:
• This activity may require older or more experienced students to operate the equipment.
• Find out if you have any experts in the class who can be in charge.

You will need:
• Thinking hats cards or wheel
• An older buddy class to help out if possible
• A video camera or digital camera

Activity

★ For this activity, you will be making a short video or a big picture book about a child adjusting to a new school.

★ As a class, use the thinking hats to discuss how you can build relationships in a new school, for example:

Red hat: How would you feel? What was it like for you on your first day at school?

White hat: What information would he or she need to know to fit in?

Yellow hat: What is something positive that could happen? What are the positive things about being a new kid?

Black hat: What could go wrong? What are the negative things about being a new kid?

Blue hat: Why does a new kid need to make friends?

Green hat: Can you think of creative ways to make friends?

★ Write down your thoughts together.

★ Allocate roles to the students as follows: Photographer(s) or cameramen, actors, editors

★ Using the information from your discussion, choose one scenario and write a storyboard, for your book or video.

★ Split into groups and allocate one part of the story to each group, or work as a class.

★ Take photographs or video shots for each segment of the story and put them together with captions or narration.

★ Present your book or your video. You might like to show it to another class and talk about what you learned.

Water Wise

Teacher's Notes

Group/Class Size: Any
Duration: 20-30 minutes

Lesson Objective(s):

* Students will describe and demonstrate simple health care and safety procedures.

Learning Outcomes:

* Students will use thinking hats to discuss and draw health and safety aspects of the swimming environment.

Write your own learning outcome(s) here:

Point(s) to Ponder:

* This activity is a great lesson to do before starting the swimming season.

You will need:

* Thinking hats cards or wheel
* Access to a swimming pool
* Paper and crayons or coloured pencils

Activity

* ★ If possible, take a short class visit to your school or community swimming pool.
* ★ While you are there, draw a picture of things that are there for health and safety reasons eg. signs, fences, water wings, flotation devices or a person supervising.
* ★ Discuss health and safety at the swimming pool.
* ★ Draw or write down the names of things that can help you to be safer at the swimming pool.
* ★ Back in class, use the thinking hats to create a class mural of health and safety at the swimming pool, for example:

   Red hat: How would you feel if you had no adult around?

   White hat: What could we see there at the pool?

   Blue hat: Is swimming safe? Why do we learn to swim?

   Yellow hat: What positive safety or health things could you see?

   Black hat: What could happen if you run around the pool?

   Green hat: What could we do to improve the safety of our pool or keep ourselves safe?

Our Class Rulz!

Teacher's Notes

Group/Class Size: Any
Duration: 20-30 minutes

Lesson Objective(s):
* Students will examine how people's attitudes, values and actions contribute to healthy physical and social environments.

Learning Outcomes:
* Students will use thinking hats to discuss their responsibilities and make a set of class rules.
* Students will create a class rules display.

Write your own learning outcome(s) here:

Point(s) to Ponder:
* This display could be either a wall poster, a freeze or a hanging display.

You will need:
* Thinking hats cards or wheel
* A class photo and photos of each student
* Magazines or coloured paper
* Coloured pencils, felts or crayons

Activity

★ Using the thinking hats cards or wheel, discuss your class rules.

Yellow hat: What positive things do I want to see in the class?

Black hat: What are some negative things that we don't want to happen? What am I not allowed to do?

White hat: What areas do we need to think about? What is not safe?

Green hat: How can we be creative with our rules?

Red hat: How do you feel if somebody does . . .?

Blue hat: Why do we have class rules?

★ Choose one class rule each.

★ Cut a speech bubble out of coloured card and write your rule in the bubble (or get the teacher to help you).

★ Stick a photo of each student with their speech bubble and make a classroom display.

★ Be creative!

Pick a Path

Teacher's Notes

Group/Class Size: Any
Duration: 15-20 minutes

Lesson Objective(s):

- Students will demonstrate ways of maintaining and enhancing relationships between individuals and with groups.

Learning Outcomes:

- Students will explore how different actions affect others using thinking hats.

Write your own learning outcome(s) here:

Point(s) to Ponder:

- Depending on how much time you have, you could also create paths to consequences that result from each choice.

You will need:

- Thinking hats cards or wheel
- A selection of scenario card (see below)
- A selection of choice cards (see below)
- A roll of paper

Activity

- ★ Choose a scenario from the following or make up your own on scenario cards:

  1. Your best friend told you "I don't want to play with you anymore".

  2. You can cheat in a game.

  3. Someone calls you a name that isn't nice.

  4. Someone takes your pencil.

  5. You leave your lunch at home.

- ★ Choose one person to pick a scenario card.

- ★ Using string, make several small paths from the person leading to different choice cards.

- ★ Write 'choice cards' based on the 'scenario cards' chosen.

- ★ Student walks along a path and picks up the choice card.

- ★ Read the card.

- ★ Use the thinking hats to discuss where this choice could lead and how it might affect friends, teachers and family.

Wish You Were Here

Teacher's Notes

Group/Class Size: Any
Duration: 15-20 minutes over a series of 4 lessons after a field trip.

Lesson Objective(s):
* Students will demonstrate knowledge and understandings of why particular places are important for people.

Learning Outcomes:
* Students will use thinking hats to aid discussion and inquiry about a particular place that they have visited.
* Students will make postcards to demonstrate their knowledge and understandings of a particular place and what it means to people.

Write your own learning outcome(s) here:

Point(s) to Ponder:
* This activity should extend over a series of 4 lessons, to allow students time to discuss the trip and design and edit their postcards.
* You might like to take photos or draw pictures to help you remember what you did.

You will need:
* Thinking hats cards or wheel
* Parent helpers
* Postcard size cardboard
* Permission to go on a field trip
* A tour guide if available
* Crayons, coloured pencils and felt pens
* A camera if available

Activity

★ As a class, decide on a local place that you would like to visit. This could be a natural or cultural location, such as a mountain, park, museum, art gallery, woodland or forest.

★ Plan a field trip to this location, keeping your lesson objective in mind.

★ Once you have completed the field trip, use the thinking hats to discuss what the place means to different people and why.

★ Some thinking hats questions might be:

Red hat: How would you feel if you lived there or you lived close by?

White hat: What information did we learn about this place? Who is it important to?

Yellow hat: What do you like about this place? What is special about it for you or others?

Black hat: What is not so positive about this place? The location? The surroundings?

Blue hat: Why is this place important to different groups? To your country?

Green hat: Would you make any changes to this place? How could this place be used differently?

★ Collate your findings into a multi-coloured chart with key words and display where everyone can see it.

★ Using the information in the class display, create postcards to a friend or relative from this place.

★ Draw a picture of the place on one side and write your letter on the other.

★ Send them to another class or to your friends.

★ If you don't want to send them, they will still make a great class display!

Time Capsule

Teacher's Notes

Group/Class Size: Any
Duration: 20-30 minutes over 2-4 lessons.

Lesson Objective(s):

*   Students will demonstrate knowledge and understandings of ways in which time and change affect people.

Learning Outcomes:

*   Students will use thinking hats to discuss the ways in which time and change have affected the society that they live in.
*   Students will look at artefacts from different eras, such as photos and discuss how society has changed over time.
*   Students will create a time capsule of items that reflect present society.

Write your own learning outcome(s) here:

You will need:

*   Thinking hats cards or wheel
*   A large, sealable container
*   Artefacts from a past era such as photos, clothes, music and household items
*   Artefacts from the present

Activity

*   ★ Make up a time capsule from a past era that reflects ways in which society has changed over time.
*   ★ Bury or hide the time capsule with a note from a fictional person, describing the time they live in for future generations. (This works best when all the items are from one era, but you could use artefacts from several eras.)
*   ★ Pull out items one at a time and read the note.
*   ★ Use the thinking hats to discuss what the objects show us about how society has changed.
*   ★ Some examples of thinking hat questions:
    Yellow hat: Why do you think wearing that would be positive?
    Black hat: Do you think it would be hard to use?
    White hat: What can we see in this photo?
    Red hat: How would you feel if you were this girl in the photo?
    Green hat: What do you think this was used for?
*   ★ This could be repeated for different eras.
*   ★ Next, make your own time capsule for future generations.
*   ★ Bring to school an item that is modern or made now. Using thinking hats, discuss how it is typical of the time you live in.
*   ★ Write a letter as a class and put it along with your objects into the container.
*   ★ You may even like to bury it somewhere.

Production Line

Teacher's Notes

Group/Class Size: Any
Duration: 15-20 minutes, over 1–2 lessons

Lesson Objective(s):

*   Students will demonstrate knowledge and understanding of how people participate in the production process.

Learning Outcomes:

*   Students will use thinking hats to increase their understanding of the production process.
*   Students will make a giant flow chart that shows their understanding of how people participate in the production process.

Write your own learning outcome(s) here:

Point(s) to Ponder:

*   You might like to get a special guest to come and speak to the class, for example, a farmer, supermarket worker of manufacturer.

You will need:

*   Thinking hats cards or wheel
*   Internet access if available
*   Information about the product and the process involoved in producing it
*   A supermarket product from a large manufacturer
*   Large sheets of paper

Activity

*   ★ Choose a well known supermarket food product to research, such as canned soup or cereal.
*   ★ As a class, research the process involved in making this product, from growing produce, right through to your parents doing their grocery shoping.
*   ★ You may wish to go on a trip to one of the places if time and money allow, such as the supermarket or a farm. Your could also invite special guest to talk to the class.
*   ★ Use the thinking hats to discuss different aspects of the production process.
*   ★ Some thinking hats questions might be:

    White hat: What facts do we know about this product? What is it made of? What does the packaging look like?

    Yellow hat: Do you like the packaging? Why is this product better than other brands?

    Red hat: How would you feel if nobody wanted to buy your product? Do you think your Mum would want to buy this product for you?

    Black hat: What do you dislike about this product?

    Green hat: How could you make it better? What could you change?

    Blue hat: Discuss concepts such as production. Who benefits the most from this product and why?

*   ★ Cut the large sheets of paper into large boxes or strips the length of the wall. Cut out some arrows and make a large flow chart.
*   ★ Write and draw you findings onto the flow chart with who is involved at each part of the production process of this product and where it ends up.
*   ★ Draw pictures such as the farmer, the supermarket checkout, your Mum and eating the final product.
*   ★ Display your chart.

Groups Galore

Teacher's Notes

Subject: Geography
PHSE and Citizenship   **Year:** 2

Group/Class Size: Any
Duration: 15-20 minutes

Lesson Objective(s):

* Students will demonstrate knowledge and understandings of how and why groups are organized within communities and societies.

Learning Outcomes:

* Students will use thinking hats to discuss how and why they are in different groups in their community and society.
* Students will make a graphic organizer of all of the groups they belong to as a class.

Write your own learning outcome(s) here:

You will need:

* Thinking hats cards or wheel
* A small photo of each student and the teacher
* Blu-tac or sticky tape
* A large sheet of paper or wall space
* Circle shapes

Activity

★ Photocopy the photos so that each student has 10 or more small photos of themselves. (Passport sized photos are good.)

★ Using the thinking hats, discuss groups in society.

★ Some thinking hat questions might be:

White hat: What groups can we think of?

Yellow hat: What is positive about being in a family?

Black hat: Are there any groups that you wouldn't want to join?

Green hat: Can you invent any new groups?

Red hat: How does it feel to be a part of a group?

Blue hat: Why do we have groups in society?

★ Using the circles as a template, draw and label different groups such as cultural or family on the board or a large piece of paper.

★ Take turns at sticking your photo up into each group circle that you are a part of.

★ Talk about which groups have more photos and why.

Story Caterpillar

Teacher's Notes

Subject: English: Writing
Year: 1

Group/Class Size: Any
Duration: 15-20 minutes

Lesson Objective(s):
- Students should write on a variety of topics, beginning to shape ideas.

Learning Outcomes:
- Students will use thinking hats to shape ideas in a class story caterpillar.

Write your own learning outcome(s) here:

You will need:
- Thinking hats cards or wheel
- Coloured paper or cardboard

Activity

★ Cut out the shape of a large caterpillar from coloured paper or card.

★ Make sure the caterpillar has a head, a large body (of several parts) and a tail.

★ Rule lines on each part for writing the story.

★ Write each part of the story (beginning, middle and end) as a class, using the thinking hats as a guide as follows:

White hat: An event (give some known details or information).

Yellow hat: Something positive happens to someone.

Black hat: A problem or a disaster that happens to someone.

Green hat: Think of something really different or creative that could happen.

Red hat: Focus on a character and how they are feeling about something.

Blue hat: What is the story about?

★ Read the story out together and talk about whether it fits together from beginning to end.

★ Now you might want to try and write your own!

Colour Match

Teacher's Notes

Group/Class Size: Any
Duration: 15-20 minutes

Lesson Objective(s):

- Reading visual and dramatic texts, including static and moving images, students should respond to meaning and ideas.

Learning Outcomes:

- Students will respond to simple coloured visuals by matching them with the corresponding words on the hats.

Write your own learning outcome(s) here:

Point(s) to Ponder:

- This is an ideal way of introducing thinking hats to your students, and it makes a great display!
- You can modify the vocabulary for your students by making your own word and picture cards.
- The activity below could also make a great art activity, such as creating patterns or collage on colour themes.

You will need:

- Thinking hat template
- Words cards
- Colour pictures (to be made as per instructions below)
- Pictures from magazines, showing people in everyday activities – such as washing the car, playing a sport, family dinner, birthday etc.

Activity

- ★ Photocopy the word and picture cards (page 27 and top half of page 28).

- ★ Cut them out and colour the pictures in.

- ★ You may like to laminate the words and pictures for future use.

- ★ You can also use pictures or graphics cut out of magazines or greetings cards.

- ★ Photocopy a set of the thinking hats templates and colour them in the appropriate colours.

- ★ Stick the thinking hats templates at the front of the class.

- ★ Play a match game with the pictures and words and stick them onto the hats students decide is most appropriate. Some may have differing viewpoints. Get them to justify their answer.

feelings	creative	sad
happy	sunshine	black
red	yellow	white
blue	green	tree
grow	facts	

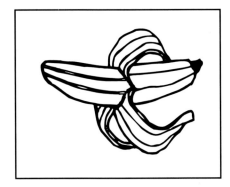  

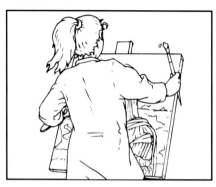

The Missing Kitten

Misty is a Persian kitten. We got her from the lady next door when she was only one week old. It was a misty morning when we got her and that is how she got her name. She has big brown eyes, and a white mark on her left ear.(1)

When Mum told me we were getting a kitten, I was so excited. I almost cried because I had never had a pet of my own before. (2)

When my neighbour dropped her off to our house, she had a beautiful red ribbon tied around her neck and my neighbour wished me happy birthday. I think this was the best birthday I have ever had. (3)

Every morning after that, Misty would jump up onto my bed and wake me up. Until one morning, when she never came. It was Saturday, and I didn't wake up until late. I went to look for her, but her basket was empty. (4)

I went and told Mum that Misty was missing, and I was so worried. (5) What if a dog from down the street had taken her away?

I searched under the coffee table. No Misty. In the lounge in her favourite spot. No Misty. Dad looked worried now too. (6) Then we heard Mum calling from the washing line. "I think you might want to come and see this." There, cuddled up and purring all snugly in the laundry basket with the fuzzy socks was a small, furry ball. "Misty!" I picked her up and gave her a great big cuddle.

"I think we should call her Socks!" said Dad. (7)

The Missing Kitten

Subject: English: Reading

Year: 2

Teacher's Notes

Group/Class Size: Any
Duration: 15-20 minutes

Lesson Objective(s):

* Students should respond to language, meanings, and ideas in different texts, relating them to personal experiences.

Learning Outcomes:

* Students will listen to a story and respond to the meaning, using thinking hats.

Write your own learning outcome(s) here:

You will need:

* Thinking hats key words
* *The Missing Kitten* story (bottom half of page 28)
* Crayons in thinking hat colors
* Paper

Activity

★ Give each student a piece of paper and one crayon in each of the thinking hat colors.

★ Stick the thinking hats key words up on coloured card at the front where everyone can see them.

★ Read the story on page 28 aloud and stop at the intervals marked. Refer to the thinking hat key words as needed.

★ Students: Write down the numbers 1–7 in the colour that matches that part of the story. The answers are at the bottom of the story.

★ How did you score?

Quick Fire

Teacher's Notes

Group/Class Size: Any/small groups
Duration: 15-20 minutes

Lesson Objective(s):

* Students will converse, ask questions, and talk about events and personal experiences in a group.

Learning Outcomes:

* Students will talk about personal experiences in a group using the thinking hats.

Write your own learning outcome(s) here:

You will need:

* Thinking hats cards or wheel
* Minute timers
* Sentence starters on cards (see below)

Activity

* Put the following sentence starters onto coloured cards (for each thinking hat):

    Red Hat: I feel . . . when . . .

    Yellow Hat: I like . . . because . . .

    Black Hat: I don't like . . . because . . .

    Green Hat: What if . . .

    White Hat: Did you know that . . .

* Split the class into small groups.

* Make several sets of the cards and give one set to each group.

* Each person has one minute to speak to the rest of the group using one of the cards.

* Pick a sentence starter out of a hat.

* Choose someone to time for one minute.

* Try to talk for one minute without stopping or saying "um".

Desert Island

Subject: Design and Technology

Year: 1

Teacher's Notes

Group/Class Size: Any/3 groups
Duration: 15-20 minutes

Lesson Objective(s):
* Within a range of technological areas and contexts, students should share ideas about the ways in which familiar technologies affect their lives.

Learning Outcomes:
* Students will discuss and think about what life is like with and without various household appliances.

Write your own learning outcome(s) here:

You will need:
* Thinking hats cards or wheel
* A selection of small household gadgets, such as can openers, knives and forks etc.

Activity

★ Split into three groups. Give each group a small gadget and a thinking hats wheel or set of cards.

★ Discuss how the object affects you and what would happen if you were stuck on a desert island without one, by going round the group, using the thinking hats as a guide.

★ Discuss one object together as a class first.

Yellow hat: Why do you like having a . . .?

Black hat: What would be the disadvantages of not having one?

Red hat: How do you think it would feel if . . .?

White hat: How does it work? What does it do?

Green hat: Can you think of any different uses?

Blue hat: What is technology? Why is it important?

★ Share your answers together and maybe make a display about what you learned.

Tool Box

Teacher's Notes

Group/Class Size: Any/in groups
Duration: 20-30 minutes

Lesson Objective(s):

* Within a range of technological areas and contexts, students should share ideas about how a particular group of people carry out technological activities.

Learning Outcomes:

* Students will discuss and explore how builders carry out technological activities using a toolbox, a guest builder and thinking hats.
* Students will discuss how different tools are used in technological activities on a building site using thinking hats.
* Students will draw and label different tools from a toolbox and how they are used in technological activities.

Write your own learning outcome(s) here:

Point(s) to Ponder:

* You may like to include a field trip to a building site.
* There are health and safety issues when using tools, so choose them wisely.
* Power tools should be used by adults only.
* All handling of tools should be supervised at all times.
* You may wish to split the class into groups, depending on their abilities.

You will need:

* Thinking hats cards or wheel
* A guest builder (or someone in costume)
* A toolbox with an assortment of tools (not a loaded nail gun please)
* Drawing paper and crayons

Activity

* ★ Role play the use of the tools in the tool box either with a special guest builder or a convincing actor.

* ★ Break out the thinking hats cards or wheel to discuss how each tool is used and why. It might be helpful to ask questions of the builder character about each tool.

* ★ Some helpful thinking hats questions might be:

    Yellow hat: What is useful about this tool or the advantages?

    Black hat: What are the negative things about this tool?

    White hat: Can you think of any other uses for this tool? What is it made of?

    Blue hat: What is a tool? What is technology? Why do we need tools?

* ★ Choose one tool each and draw it in the middle of a piece of paper.

* ★ Write the name of the tool at the top of the page.

* ★ It would be helpful to have a list of the tool names on the board for copying.

* ★ Go around the class and talk about the tool you chose.

* ★ Display your pictures as a class.

Transport Me!

Teacher's Notes

Group/Class Size: Any/3 groups
Duration: 20-30 minutes

Lesson Objective(s):

* Within a range of technological areas and contexts, students should explore and compare the roles of some examples of technology in daily life in their own and another time or place.

Learning Outcomes:

* Students will use thinking hats to explore and compare transportation technology in the past, present and future.
* Students will make a class big book about transportation through the ages.

Write your own learning outcome(s) here:

You will need:

* Thinking hats cards or wheel
* Pictures, books and text about different forms of transport

Activity

★ Use thinking hats and resources to discuss how transport is a form of technology and how it has changed from past, present and future.

★ Some examples of thinking hats questions:

White hat: What kinds of transport did they use in the past? (Guess and reveal.) How does it work? What is it called?

Black hat: What would be the negatives about that kind of transport?

Yellow hat: What do you like about this kind of transport?

Red hat: How would you feel if you had to use that?

Green hat: Can you think of a new transport technology? What do you think they might have in the future?

Blue hat: How is transport a form of technology?

★ Split into three groups – past, present and future.

★ In each group, draw and write about transport technology in that period of time.

★ Compile your information into a class book.

Load of Rubbish!

Teacher's Notes

Subject: Design and Technology
Science   **Year:** 2

Group/Class Size: Any
Duration: 20-30 minutes – series of 3 lessons.

Lesson Objective(s):

- Within a range of technological areas and contexts, students should produce technological solutions. They will gather information, and identify and discuss needs, opportunities, and preferences in their local environment.

Learning Outcomes:

- Students will use thinking hats to identify and discuss rubbish disposal in their local area and associated technologies.
- Students will identify problems with current technologies and discuss needs, identifying technological solutions.
- Students will draw or design a solution to a specific problem with rubbish disposal.

Write your own learning outcome(s) here:

You will need:

- Thinking hats cards or wheel
- Information/resources about local rubbish disposal
- Paper and crayons

Activity

- ★ Take a walk around the rubbish bins in your neighbourhood or take a trip to a waste disposal area or dump.
- ★ Think of answers to thinking hats questions, like:

    White hat: What can you see? How does this work? What are the facts?

    Yellow hat: What are the positive things about this technology? What do you like about it?

    Black hat: What needs improving? What are the problems that you can see?

    Green hat: What happens to the rubbish next? What alternatives can you think of? Can you think of a creative solution for the rubbish problem?

    Red hat: How do you feel about this? How would you feel if this happened?

- ★ Make a list of problems with the current technology on the board.
- ★ As a class or in groups, vote on a problem that you want to work on to find a solution.
- ★ Make a list of all the aspects of the problem, including:

    Key words, People who need to help, Where to start, What you will need, Cost/Budget

- ★ Start to work on a solution.
- ★ See if you can put your plan into action!
- ★ Display what you have learned as a class.

Creative Numbers

Subject: Mathematics: Number

Year: 1

Teacher's Notes

Group/Class Size: Any
Duration: 15-20 minutes

Lesson Objective(s):
- Within a range of meaningful contexts, students should be able to rote count to at least 50.

Learning Outcomes:
- Students will make a creative class display of numbers 1–50 and count them as a class.

Write your own learning outcome(s) here:

You will need:
- Green thinking hat or green thinking hat card
- Numbers 1–50 with names on cards or on the board
- Paper, crayons, coloured pencils, or paint
- Art supplies: Magazines to cut out, glitter, pipe-cleaners, sequins, material scraps etc.
- Glue

Activity

★ Choose one number each. (If you are a fast worker you could choose more than one.)

★ On a piece of paper, think of the most creative way of displaying the number. (Wear your green hat.)

★ Write the name of the number in the centre of a piece of paper.

★ Decorate it creatively. Use your imagination.

★ As a class, discuss any groups that match the numbers you know of, such as eggs in packs of 6 or 12.

★ Make a hanging or display with your numbers and practise until you can recognise any of the numbers.

Number Stories = Fun

Teacher's Notes

Group/Class Size: Any, work in pairs.
Duration: 15-20 minutes

Lesson Objective(s):
* Within a range of meaningful contexts, students should be able to write number sentences using =, from story contexts.

Learning Outcomes:
* Students will use thinking hats to write a simple story for their partners, that makes a number sentence, using =.
* Students will listen to their partner's story and work out and write down the number sentence for the story.

Write your own learning outcome(s) here:

You will need:
* Thinking hats cards or wheel
* Paper and pencils

Activity

* ★ Working in pairs, choose one partner to make up a story and one partner to work out the number sentence using numbers 1–10 and either plus or minus.

* ★ Choose a thinking hat to base the story on. Here are some examples:

    Black hat: Something that was lost (- equation)

    Yellow hat: Something gained/found (+ equation)

    Green hat: Be as creative as possible (An alien discovered 2 more humans living underground.)

    Red hat: A feeling (It was a happy day when we got 3 new kittens . . .)

* ★ Tell the story to your partner and write down the number sentence as an equation. You can use the words to help you eg. 2 ducks and 1 duck = 3 ducks.

* ★ Swap around and have a go!

* ★ Choose some pairs to share their stories with the class.

It Will Never Happen!

123

Subject: Mathematics: Handling Data

Teacher's Notes

Year: 2

Group/Class Size: Any
Duration: 15-20 minutes

Lesson Objective(s):
* Within a range of meaningful contexts, students should be able to compare familiar or imaginary, but related, events and order them on a scale of least likely to most likely.

Learning Outcomes:
* Students will discuss the probability of familiar or imaginary events using thinking hats.
* Students will create a long chart and stick pictures of events ordering them to show how likely or unlikely they are to happen.

Write your own learning outcome(s) here:

You will need:
* Thinking hats cards or wheel
* Pictures showing a range of events: real, imaginary, fantasy etc. (These could put on card if they are going to be used again.)
* A way of attaching the pictures to the chart
* Large sheets of paper joined together to make a long wall chart

Activity

123

★ Using thinking hats, discuss different events and why they are likely or unlikely to occur. Include whether they have occurred in the past or are likely to occur in the future.

★ Some suggestions:

Green hat: What is something weird/wacky/imaginative that might never happen?

Yellow hat: What is something that will probably happen/never happen and is therefore positive?

Black hat: What is something that will probably happen/never happen and is therefore negative?

White hat: What has happened before?

Red hat: How would you feel if this happened/never happened?

★ As a class, look at the cards with different events on them, and discuss the probability of the event. (also past and future)

★ Stick them on the correct place on the chart; most unlikely at one end to most likely at the other.

★ Select a picture on the chart when it's finished and make a statement about how probable the event is.

Once Upon a Time

Subject: Mathematics: Shape, space and measures

Year: 2

Teacher's Notes

Group/Class Size: Any
Duration: 15-20 minutes

Lesson Objective(s):

* Within a range of meaningful contexts, students should be able to read time and know the units of time: minute, hour, day, week, month and year.

Learning Outcomes:

* Students will use thinking hats to write a story as a class that includes all of the above units of time.

Write your own learning outcome(s) here:

You will need:

* Thinking hats cards or wheel
* Large sheets of paper
* Felt pens

Activity

★ Use the thinking hats to write a story as a class on large paper and leave gaps for the unit words, using them in any order; for example it was 15 _____ past 4 in the afternoon of _____ the third of _____ _____.

★ Thinking hats suggestions:

Yellow hat: Something positive happens.

Black hat: A disaster, a problem or something negative.

Red hat: How does a character feel?

White hat: What happens next?

Green hat: Something creative or strange that happens.

★ Read the story as a class, and fill in the blanks.

Shape Up or Ship Out!

Subject: Science: Physical Processes

Year: 1

Teacher's Notes

Group/Class Size: Any
Duration: 15-20 minutes

Lesson Objective(s):

* Students can share and compare their emerging science ideas.

Learning Outcomes:

* Students will discuss and experiment with sinking and floating, using thinking hats to share and compare their ideas.

Write your own learning outcome(s) here:

You will need:

* Thinking hats cards or wheel
* A selection of small objects
* A tank of water

Activity

* ★ Using thinking hats, share ideas about floating and sinking.

* ★ Some suggestions:

    White hat: What objects sink/float that we already know about?

    Yellow hat: Why is floating a good thing?

    Black hat: What would happen if it didn't float? Why does this not float? What might make it sink?

    Blue hat: What is floating and sinking?

* ★ Test the objects out and talk about your ideas as to why objects might float and others sink.

Changing Places

Teacher's Notes

Group/Class Size: Any
Duration: 20-30 minutes – lesson series

Lesson Objective(s):

* Students can suggest ways that their immediate physical environment was different in the past.

Learning Outcomes:

* Students will use thinking hats and resources to discuss ways in which the school land or environment has changed over the years.
* Students will make a short presentation about the past, present and future of a part of their school environment.

Write your own learning outcome(s) here:

You will need:

* Thinking hats cards or wheel
* Resources, photos or guest speakers
* A camera (if available)

Activity

★ Choose a part of the school environment, such as the school field.

★ Go there and take photos of the physical environment.

★ Using the thinking hats, discuss current uses of the environment.

★ Some suggestions:

White hat: What can you see? What do we use this place for?

Black hat: What needs improving? What negative things do people do to this environment?

Yellow hat: What do you like about this place?

Green hat: What creative uses could you think of for this space?

★ Use resources such as the Internet, books or photos to explore changes in the environment over time.

★ Discuss, using thinking hats.

★ Make a display to present to another class.

Seasons

Teacher's Notes

Group/Class Size: Any
Duration: 15-20 minutes

Lesson Objective(s):
* Students can investigate the responses of plants or animals, including people, to environmental changes in their habitats.

Learning Outcomes:
* Students will use thinking hats to discuss what changes take place in their environment with the seasons and how these changes affect them personally.

Write your own learning outcome(s) here:

You will need:
* Thinking hats cards or wheel
* Information/Resources about seasons
* Large paper

Activity

★ Using large paper, draw up a chart with places for the following information:

Season

Changes

Feelings/Effects on Me

★ You might like to use pictures as well.

★ Using the thinking hats, fill in the chart as a class.

★ Some suggestions:

White hat: What happens in spring? What do you see in this season?

Black hat: What do you not like about winter?

Yellow hat: What do you like about summer?

Green hat: What would happen if we didn't have seasons? Can we change seasons?

Blue hat: What are seasons? Why do we have them? What causes them?

Red hat: How do you feel when this happens?

High Tech

Teacher's Notes

Subject: Science: Materials and their Properties

Year: 2

Group/Class Size: Any
Duration: 15-20 minutes

Lesson Objective(s):

- Students can use a variety of methods to investigate different ideas about the same object or event.

Learning Outcomes:

- Students will investigate different ideas about how a simple piece of classroom technology works.
- Students will use thinking hats to discuss a piece of classroom technology.

Write your own learning outcome(s) here:

You will need:

- Thinking hats cards or wheel
- A simple classroom technology such as a stapler or pencil sharpener.

Activity

★ Using the thinking hats, think of ways to investigate an object and how it works.

★ Think about experiments, investigations or activities you could do with your object.

★ Some examples:

White hat: What does it do? What other objects does it look like? What parts does it have?

Green hat: What different uses can you think of? What creative changes could you make to the object? How could you modify it?

★ Make up a brochure with information about what you discovered.

Colour Wheel

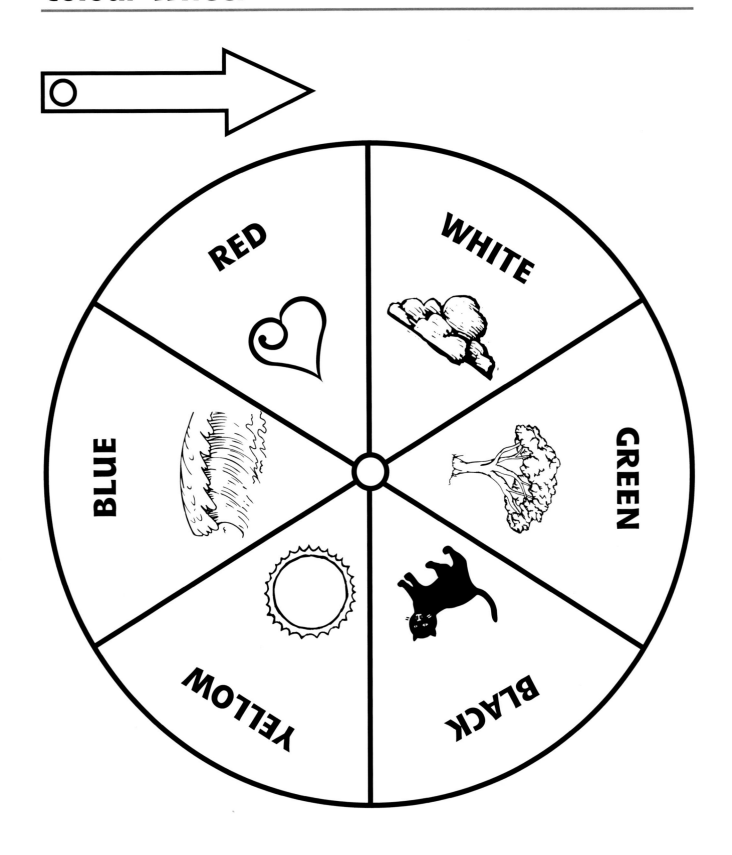

★ Colour each segment in the correct colour for each thinking hat.

★ Paste onto cardboard and cut out the two pieces.

★ Use a short pencil or stick with a point to make the wheel spinnable.

RED

Thinking Hat Cards

BLACK

Thinking Hat Cards

WHITE

Thinking Hat Cards

YELLOW

Thinking Hat Cards

GREEN

Thinking Hat Cards

BLUE

Thinking Hat Cards

Black

- What are the negative points?
- What could go wrong?
- Who might think this is a negative idea? Why?
- What don't you like about this?
- What needs to be changed or fixed?
- Who would be negatively affected?

Thinking Hat Cards

Red

- How would you feel if that was you?
- How do you think that person feels?
- What emotion can you see or hear?
- What effect would this have on the people?
- How would I feel about this in 10 years time? In 5 years?
- How would people in the past feel about this?

Thinking Hat Cards

Yellow

- What are the positive points?
- Who would agree with this? Why?
- What do we really like about this?
- What are the best parts?
- What are the benefits?
- Who would benefit?

Thinking Hat Cards

White

- What are the facts?
- How does this work?
- What do we know already about this?
- Who might know more information about this topic?
- What is it?
- What does it do?
- What is it made of?

Thinking Hat Cards

Blue

- What is the main point of this?
- What does this mean?
- Why do we need to know this?
- Why does it matter?
- Who cares?
- How does this relate to what we know about . . .?

Thinking Hat Cards

Green

- How could we do this differently?
- How could we look at this differently?
- What new ideas can you come up with?
- Can you think of a new solution?
- What if . . .?
- What might happen next?
- Where could this lead to?
- What are some other perspectives or thoughts?

Thinking Hat Cards

Thinking Hats Reference Chart

GREEN

This is such a fun hat. Think of the possibilities. Explore new heights. Question everything, turn it inside out and upside down and ask, what if? Take what you have and turn it into something new. Turn a corner or change direction. Subvert a well known idea or story. The possibilities with using the green hat are truly endless. When you have your green hat on, forget about what your mother would feel about it, forget about the facts, just jump right out of the box and see what happens. The green hat is for exploring new territory, creating and asking where to from here? Some useful visuals: A little green seedling, a tree or an expansive green field.

WHITE

When we put our white hat on, we seek out facts and information. What do we know about this already? The five senses come into play when using this hat. What can we smell/taste/hear/see? Switch your emotions off and focus on the data. Put your scientist's lab coat on (which is usually white by the way). Look at what you can observe and the evidence in front of you. Don't make a judgment on anything yet. Just gather, calculate and measure. Some helpful visuals: A white lab coat, a blank canvas or a fresh white piece of paper.

RED

The Red hat is based on feelings and emotions. Discuss how each person would feel and why. Put facts out of the picture and look at the effect on a person emotionally, spiritually or socially. Delve deeper and ask questions about values and beliefs and how situations affect people differently, depending on their upbringing, personal characteristics or circumstances. Some helpful visuals are: Hearts (linked to love, romance and affection and also anger and danger) or a red flag, seeing red.

BLUE

Take all the things you have learned from using the other 5 hats, and gather them up in a big, blue bag. This is what the blue hat is all about. What are the ties that bind everything together? Sum up your argument or your findings. Look at the bigger picture. How does this relate to us in the country we live in or even to the human race? What themes can we make out of all of this? Why do we even need to know this? What is the point of all of it? If you are in a philosophical mood, the blue hat may be just what you need. Some helpful visuals: A blue sky (arches over everything), a wave.

YELLOW

This hat looks at the world through rose-tinted glasses. What sets you alight or lights you up? Take a look at the funny, sunny side with this hat, and forget your cares. Be an optimist for a day and explore what you enjoy and what makes the world a better place. Why do some people like things that others can't stand? Ask yourself why you like what you do and why it has such a positive effect on you. Useful visuals: Sunshine, sunflowers, a smiley face. Key words are: Excellent! Positive! Fantastic!

BLACK

The black hat is essentially a pessimist's hat. This will never work! Sometimes we need a dose of reality before we plough ahead. When we have the black hat on we look at what could go wrong and who may be affected negatively. What do we dislike about this? What needs improvement or just that extra something? Feel free to be the judge when you wear this hat, just be careful you don't hurt anybody's feelings! Why do some people dislike things that others just love? Explore the realms of the negative, the ugly and the downright horrible. Find out the often unrevealed details and put them on display. Some helpful pictures: A judge in a black robe, the grim reaper, a witch's hat.

Hat Template

Thinking Hats – Key Words

argument	what	facts	opinion	happy	assess
who	information	view	when	thinking	decision
feeling	evidence	debate	sad	messages	why

Thinking Hats – Key Words

positive	knowledge	emotion	empathy	alternative	ideas
values	where	negative	research	effect	judge
discovery	consequence	understand	solution	creativity	data